MOZART

CONCERTO No. 4

in D major—K. 218

FOR VIOLIN AND PIANO

Edited and provided with Cadenzas
by JOSEPH JOACHIM

Published in 2019 by Allegro Editions

Concerto No. 4 for Violin and Piano
ISBN: 978-1-9748-9992-0 (paperback)

Cover design by Kaitlyn Whitaker

Cover image: "Violin Front View Isolated on White" by AGCuesta, courtesy of Shutterstock;
"Black and White Piano Keys" by Nerthuz, courtesy of iStock;
"Music Sheet" by danielo, courtesy of Shutterstock

ALLEGRO EDITIONS

CONCERTO No. 4
K. 218

Edited by JOSEPH JOACHIM

W. A. MOZART
(1756-1791)

CADENZA by JOACHIM
SOLO

CADENZA by JOACHIM

18

24

CADENZA by JOACHIM

CONCERTO No. 4

in D major, for Violin and Piano

PART FOR VIOLIN

with Cadenzas by Joseph Joachim

CONCERTO No. 4
K. 218

Edited by JOSEPH JOACHIM

VIOLIN

W.A. MOZART
(1756-1791)

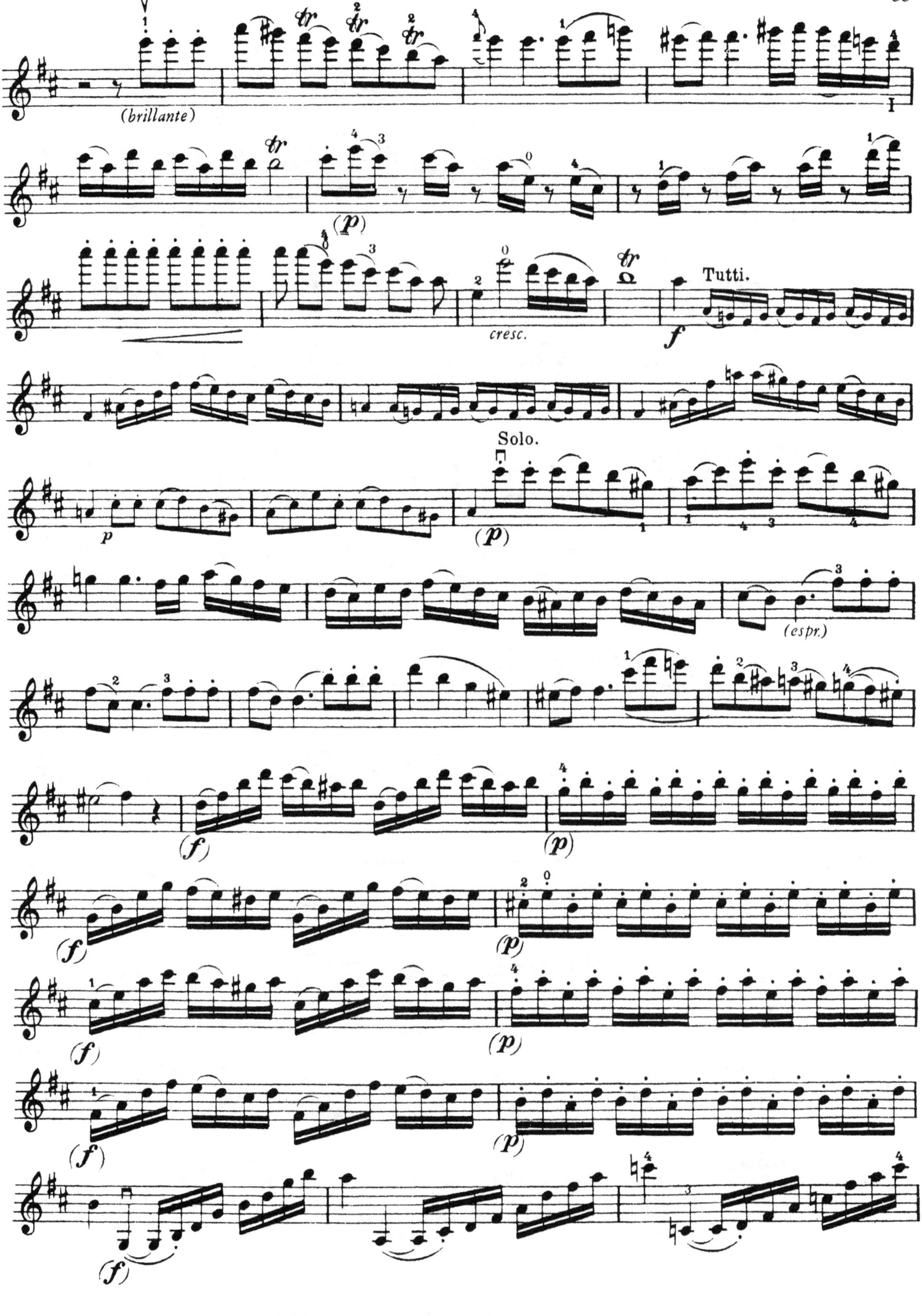
(brillante)
cresc.
Tutti.
Solo.
(espr.)

34

CADENZA by JOACHIM

Andante grazioso

Allegro ma non troppo

www.ingramcontent.com/pod-product-compliance
Lightning Source LLC
LaVergne TN
LVHW061344060426
835512LV00016B/2664